# The Horns of Taurus by J Griffyth Fairfax

James Griffyth Fairfax was born on 15th July 1886 in Sydney, Australia.

Fairfax, a great-grandson of the Australian newspaper tycoon John Fairfax, was educated in England at Winchester School and then New College, Oxford.

His first volume of poetry, 'The Gates of Sleep & Other Poems', was published in 1906. He was an active member of literary circles and especially of poets such as Ezra Pound, who each went on to influence the other.

Fairfax joined the British Army and served in the 15th Indian Division for the entirety of the Great War, and reached the rank of Captain.

As well as being known as a translator Fairfax occasionally still published volumes of poetry; 'The Horns of Tarus' (1914), 'The Temple of Janus' (1917) and 'Mesopotamia: Sonnets and Lyrics at Home and Abroad' (1919).

Fairfax was elected for the Conservative and Unionist party to the House of Commons in the 1924 election representing the borough constituency of Norwich until the 1929 election.

James Griffyth Fairfax died at the age of 89 in France on 27th January 1976.

## Index of Contents

I0158373

ON A COLOUR-PRINT BY TORII KIYONAGA
CAMARADERIE
AMOUR VOYAGEUR
BUDDHA
RONDEL FOR THE NIGHT


THE HORNS OF TAURUS

ANNUNICATION

To MRS ALFRED FOWLER

Blossom of almond, bright against the blue
Of spring seas, spring skies, shining thy fair hope
Which ever flowers when the months renew

Life out of this gray sleep wherein we grope,
When Winter makes us moles: this, dreamed afar
Suddenly widens the down-narrowed scope,

And Life looks out as one who sees a star
Burn solitary on dark-breasted Night,
Or, to one drowning, thou the saving spar,

Drifted toward him in the storm's despite,
Seemest, and all the massed despairs recede
From the coast rising up a line of light.

Blossom of almond, what fair fancies feed
Upon thy petalled sweetness, clustering bees,
Drunk with the splendour of each golden deed

The yield of thine o'erbrimming treasuries!
Out on what voyage sails the questing mind
Launching for galleon on charmed seas

Thy pale chalice with a favouring wind
Blowing on lawns Elysian, land-locked bays
Where sleep Hyperion's proud coursers find,

And Argo's keel peace of foam-'wildered ways.
Blossom of almond, what dreams, given wings,
Float in the air a-quiver to thy sprays,

And what a scarlet song Adventure sings,
Who soars and hovers and lets music slip
Between unthrifty fingers! Such sound springs

When from a wakened fountain waters drip
Silver flute-notes upon wet porphyry,
And slumber leaves the nymphs. So doth outstrip

Slow thoughts of Winter, Spring whose feet are free,
Shod with the sandals of her young desire.
A laggard of a leaden tread goes he,

The spouse of darkness: her, the bride of fire,
We, with a voice too faltering pursue,
Save thou wilt lend thy lightness to our lyre,
Blossom of almond, bright against the blue.


## BELL' ANDARE

To DOROTHY SHAKESPEAR

I

Over the river
Very softly the owls are calling;
Shy ripples shiver
To the sound of the smooth oars falling;
The moon-glade follows our wake
Like a dwindling silver snake;
Gray shadows quiver
Where the drowning arms of the willows shake.


II

Statelily and slow
Are gliding to and fro
Night's black swans a-row.


III

The dream-boat drifted,
Floats out on the cool tide shining;
From wet oars lifted
Long widen the water-rings twining;

Tenderly the west winds keep
Fluttering Love's lashes asleep:
Her vision shifted
Is blown in pale petals over the deep.


IV


Where seas end, and skies,
Turn our sorrowful eyes:
Dawn's white doves arise.


## PRÖSSAU IN THE RAIN


Long, long is the valley, and the clouds hang low,
Close the mist clings the dripping wood,
Wet winds swing the rowan-berries to and fro,
The fluttered spray is bright as blood.

Tawny is the mountain torrent, branch and weed
Rise and rush past, and drown, and rise:
Red rock and gray rock the bewildering speed
Spurns, and the dun foam bursts and flies.

Music, shrill music, mounts to a muffled sky,
Fall the echoes on drenching ground.
Divined, desired, as of world-old pipes blown by,
Haunting, summoning, floats a sound.

Not alone, alone, go I the wildwood way;
Here, though all voice of man be dumb,
Powers of cloud, rain, river I call to-day,
Powers and Presences hear and come.


## ZOCODOVER


Splendid light, through the time-defying arches,
Falls on the sinister square:
The ghost of the swordsman, balladist, dreamer marches;
Cervantes stands at the stair.

The cringing rabble, beggarly, sordid faces,
Break in a scurrying cloud;
His soul's shame for their great, degraded races

He voices, lonely, aloud.

*TOLBDO, 1912.*


## BACCHANALIA

### To PEGGY MCARTHUR

Lo, the speed of the flying seasons
Scatters abroad from the beechen branches
Brown and gold:
Wind in a league with Autumn's treasons
Blows upon aspens light and blanches
Leaves a-cold.

Over the wavered meadows shaken,
Over the grasses bent and bending,
Glide and glance
Wild Bacchantes whose feet awaken
From the slumber of Summer's sending
Autumn's dance.

Bright as a flame and light as laughter,
Out upon windy ways they follow,
Shade and shine,
Him whose music, before and after,
Lingers in woodland height and hollow,
Pan divine!


## THE STREAM OF STARS

### A CHINESE LEGEND

### To WYN LAIDLEY

**Kien-Niu,**
Sky-flower, sky-flower, Seventh Moon,
Cradle-crescent softly swayed,
Blossom into beauty soon,
Light thy swinging lamp of jade!

Swallows, bridge the sorrow-laden
Stream of stars for Spinning-Maiden!

**Spinning-Maiden.**

Seventh moon, and seventh eve,
Heaven-given night draw near
Souls that being severed grieve
All the lone and loveless year!

Build a bridge of feathers blue,
Swallows, build for K'ien Niu!

**K'ien-Niu.**

In between the cloudy bars,
Pitiless and pale and wide
Swims the river of the stars;
Waves of mocking light divide.

Swallows, bridge the sorrow-laden
Stream of stars for Spinning-Maiden!

**Spinning-Maiden.**

Sudden sounds have filled the air;
Ah, the hurried whirr of wings!
Look, across the gulf, Despair,
New the path of pleasure springs!

Build a bridge of feathers blue,
Swallows, build for K'ien Niu!

**K'ien Niu.**

Fate becomes a loving friend
Once a year, and once alone:
See the solemn goddess bend
Smiling with a face of stone!

"Cross the river sorrow-laden,
K'ien Niu and Spinning-Maiden!"

*NOTE. The shepherd and the spinning-girl are two stars doomed by the gods to live on opposite sides of the Milky Way. On the seventh night of the seventh month in each year birds form a bridge across the "River of Stars," allowing the lovers to meet.*

DUNVEGAN

To L. C. MACKINNON

The purple of the heather floods mine eyes,

Deeper than any seas,
Any skies;
That glory was not of the Tyrian dyes.

Away in the red West, old towers rise;
While the sun kindles these
When he dies,
He cannot burn the purple from mine eyes.

Far off a hawk hovers, a curlew cries;
Now, though a little breeze
Softly tries,
No wind can blow the purple from mine eyes.

To a faint bell a faint echo replies;
Dark on the valley-trees
Shadow lies;
The night will come all purple to mine eyes.


DECOR

To MRS R. S. BODEN

Dim tapestries of Turkestan
Make memorable night of day
In faded crimsons of Iran,
Emerald, mellow gold, and gray.

Proud horsemen hunt the antlered deer
Through glades fantastically pale,
And moon-browed maidens stoop and peer
From slender towers, with parted veil.

On wizard rocks enchanted flower
Rich blossoms in unearthly air,
And filmy waters plunge and shower
In shaken music wild and rare.

The world is old and full of dreams,
Their fragrance delicately clings
To royal silks whose glory seems
Awake among unworthy things.


A LITTLE SONG OF COMPENSATIONS

Would you were wise as you are sweet,
O little lips that smile so much,
Have such soft kisses to repeat
And mean so little! Being such,
To blame the lightness of your touch
Were captious, dear, and indiscreet,
For Wisdom's lips smile not so much,
And wise, you would not be so sweet.


## MISCHIEF AWAY!

### To ALVARO ALCALA GALIANO Y OSMA

If Love sings in these hills I hear him never,
Far other wandering and weaving notes
Rise, halt, and fall, yet seem afloat forever
Of mountain-streams whose many silver throats
Are sounding flutes for Autumn's breath to blow.
Who would heed here the flight of Love's blind arrows?
Those of the rain more delicately go;
Who turn for sight of Cytherea's sparrows
Fluttering at the footsteps of their queen?
The little winds among the aspens playing,
Touching the green to gray, the gray to green,
Dance more delightfully on branches swaying:
We have no eyes for Eros in the wood,
Nor Aphrodite suits our listening mood.


## RHYTHMICAL PEACE

Woods, for your music all day murmuring
Between your branches, when your waters fall,
I would give all my songs that I might sing
Once with your voice, then sing no more at all.
Of my vain words, and hollow tones, my heart
Is wearied; hath one comfort of the wind?
And I would choose long silence for my part
To drive unwelcome dwellers from the mind,
Pride, that outrageous guest who all devours,
And with him in his train, a wanton knave,
Ambition brings, the spendthrift of the hours:
To such I would no longer be the slave,
       But, master in mine house, the room would fill

With your song's memory, and myself be still.


## VOX CLAMANTIS

Because of Beauty reigning in my heart,
Behold I draw the dark threads in my hand,
And shadows turn to shining by the art

Of Loveliness that comes at my command!
O clouds across the everlasting sun,
See! I have sent my winds upon the land!

Lo, on what feet of light my children run,
A crimson garland in their streaming hair,
And all their voices glorying as one!

Gray race of men who sow and reap despair,
Lift from the patient furrow prouder eyes;
Follow my swift ones who divide the air

With music thrilling as the song that flies
Of moving arrows in a frosted morn:
Then laugh! As when triumphantly arise

The banners of an army onward borne!
The sullen squadrons of the dark depart;
An eddy in the dust are those I scorn

Because of Beauty reigning in my heart.


## DIALOGUE

**The Lover**
Love, when thou earnest on triumphant wing,
Who could have dreamed thou must fare hence on foot,
Or that a weed of so much woe could spring
Where thy delightful flower alone had root!

**Love**
Lover, I have not wings mine own to wear,
Only I borrow Wisdom's in her sleep;
So when she wakes and claims again the air,
Wingless along the level ways I creep.

**The Lover**
Would I had gone with Wisdom on the wind,
Since the high voyage is not thine to lead!

**Love**
Wisdom hath many eyes, but Love is blind:
Lo, thou hast leaned upon a little reed!

**The Lover**
Dearer than Wisdom's strength thy weakness seems.

**Love**
Mine eyes are sightless, being filled with dreams.


CIUDAD DE ORO

To DOROTHEA MACKELLAR

A splendid city, like a splendid ship,
With all sail set against a western Sun,
Drives where the gray plains lift and lean and dip,
And where the sea-winds chase, long shadows run.

Glory of old Spain on a golden rock,
Proud head to carry a Castilian crown;
Thy crumbled walls hear phantom armies shock,
Shadowy warriors strike faint foemen down:

Plume, cloak, and rapier, in a flare of torches,
Flutter along the dusky-winding street,
And under proud and many-blazoned porches
Echoes a muffled tread of mailed feet.

All silent now the shielded lions, guarding,
Watch in the purple field where stars are sown;
And a sad moon, her silver veil discarding,
Sees with soft eyes a city turned to stone.

Splendours of Love and War, ancestral stories,
High passions raising life above the dust,
Oblivion, disastrous grave of glories,
Works on them, and her minions Moth and Rust.

Thy poplars, in their ghostly branches shaken,
Hear murmuring thy waters where they meet,
Eresma and Clamores, "O Forsaken!"

And "O Forsaken!" windy tongues repeat.

A splendid city, like a splendid ship,
A drifting derelict whose course is done;
Lo, they have let thy golden standard slip,
And the sea trails it to the drowning Sun!

*SEGOVIA, 1912.*


## BITTER-SWEET

What lover knows ever
If Love kisses or burns?
Spring moves in the meadow,
A witch light as a shadow,
The strange beauty returns,
Bringing the Lady of Sparrows
And the wild boy with the arrows.
No lover knows ever . . .
And no lover learns.


## REVENANT DE LA BIEN-AIMEE

Last night, when I had fallen on sleep, I dreamed
Of her return in glory who is gone;
She stood beside me and about her streamed,
Pale gold in light of a late moon that shone,
Her hair unbound; and as I looked thereon
Words she spoke tenderly whose clear sound rose
Like lute-notes from the strings Love plays upon,
Only my heart for lute my lady chose
And drew with a light kiss her music to its close.

When she had ceased, fell silence like a veil
Over us twain who gave to speech no thought,
Content, as when of old the words would fail,
Too little for Love's burden they had brought,
And some fell by the way, but we lacked naught.
So, in my dream we stayed together, still,
Counting those stars the spider Night had caught
In the grey web she weaveth of her skill;
And Time, blind thief, went by us, darkly, doing ill.

Long over us the cloud of quietness

Hung, and a thousand hours had gone their way
Into the shadowy graves that them possess,
When Dawn, pearl-sandalled at the gates of Day,
'Gan to her lips her silver clarion lay;
Then, with that sound unborn, my lady stepped
Softly toward me, but she might not say,
For all her will, one word I could have kept,
But passed like wind away, and I awoke who slept.


## CHARLES MERYON

Between the sparse and stunted trees
Tall, sordid houses block the sky,
And birds of wicked portent fly
Like lost souls in the bitter breeze.
Over the bridges, down the quays,
The busy, weird homunculi
Crawl in and out, and crawl, and die;
And Hell brings almost hope to these.

Beauty, this is thy sorcery,
At Foulness' very heart to thrive,
Then break, a radiant and live
White blossom on a withered tree;
So that the blind cry out to see,
The deaf to hear, the Gods arrive.


## SONNET

Grief that had followed in the train of Gladness
Stooped on us, hawking in a windy sky,
And down the furrows of the gray field Sadness
Love, as his fortune failed him, turned to fly.
Surely a dark star in the clouded heavens
Stood averse, and a woeful web was spun,
Though in the Sisters' hands the threads laid even
Shone bright gold when the weaving was begun.
Heavy is Sorrow in the room of Pleasure,
Moving with slow feet and earth-gazing eyes
Where, of old, Joy went tripping a light measure
And Laughter with him, a fair friend unwise.
Since to such happy union 'longs brief date
We'll throw no more the dice with crooked Fate.

## THE PURPLE HILL

Here alone on the hill in the windy weather
Here alone on the hill with a dream destroyed!
The sorrowing rain falls thick on the crouching heather,
A crying of gulls conies thinly out of the void.

How can a word help Love if his heart forsake him?
My heart is a husk tossed to and fro in the air:
But Love is dead; you may laugh, for it will not wake him,
Laugh out loud he will neither answer nor care.

Here alone on the hill; and a wind goes urging
Over the loch the mist on the mountain-brow;
Oh that a wind would rise where my thoughts are surging,
And out on the water drive them and drown them now!

Here alone on the hill with the gray loch under,
A cluster of pines, and Love's house hidden below :
Would there be sleep in those shifting waves, I wonder!
There is rest neither here nor there, let us rise and go.

Let us wander over the earth in a mask of laughter:
When the heart is empty the mouth is merry at will
But no more dreaming now and the long time after:
There was once a dream, and a house, and a purple hill.


## MADURA

### To MRS SHOLTO DOUGLAS

The moon is over Madura,
In her starry field:
She moves mirrored in the cool
Waters of the holy pool,
The moon over Madura,
Lo the golden shield!

The moon was over Madura,
Moving even so;
Through her curtained, cloudy lace
She stooped with a quiet face,
The moon over Madura
A thousand years ago.

Moon, be over Madura
Ever golden-young;
Let your roving beauty pass
Slow, slow in the hushed glass;
Moon, be over Madura
Till the last bell be rung!

## RECONTRE

Subtile, luminous grace,
In likeness of my dream's crystalline whiteness,
She, through the veil her face,
Shed as a lamp reveals its core of brightness.

Even her least word went
A spark of fire, alive, her beauty bearing;
And a divine content
Covered her like the mantle she was wearing.

Each pause her silence made,
To me was like a moon-lit meadow lying,
Where a still river strayed
And a wind went in the reeds, never sighing.

Memories moved and passed,
Stirring the fringe of Time with wings that quivered:
Rent was the veil at last;
The mirror of illusion slipped and shivered.

Clear in a space that glows,
Under a sky of starry, southern weather,
Our hands pluck Life, the rose;
The threads of our desire are drawn together.

So, in a Persian grove,
In Ispahan, the bird of sorrow singing,
Wakes the wild heart of Love,
Praises the lips and eyes and sudden clinging.

Far, so far off! Does she
Keep in the cloudy Cavern of Unknowing
A sister-dream of me,
And even dimly see our shadows going?

When I would speak to her,

My thought upon the shore of speech is broken:
Even a thought will stir
That peace from which my soul would not be woken.


## VOYAGE

Alone, in hearing of a stream
From fabled mountains full of years,
Easily, as on wings, a dream
Rises when Night's last star appears,
My spirit upward floating nears
The far-off source of silent snow
From whence those storied waters flow.

So journeying I lightly tread
The terrors blind to waking eyes
Of caves whose eerie gloom is shed
Nor noon nor eve by human skies,
And where the circling phantom flies
Of Fear whose frozen echoes pass,
Shivering, under domes of glass.

But still the stream I follow far
Up to a lost lake, sunken deep,
Whereover ancient dragons war
Among the waves that curve and sweep,
Black as the mid-night eyes of Sleep;
And the dim vault above them rings
With beating of their evil wings.

Out of the shadow of that dread,
Slowly I float until a rare
Glimmer of Heaven high overhead
Shows like a blossom, blue and fair.
Then last the solitary air
Blows keen about me and I see
Worlds dead, worlds dying, worlds to be.


## MORTIS UMBRA

The going of the Sun in gold and crimson,
The coming of the moon and many stars
Trouble my soul no more; the time is sped
When I have followed in the field red Mars,

Or lain where Eros' softer light was shed;
But gray is now the gold, and ash the crimson.

My days are ebbing down the sands of saffron,
My hours are shallow in the opal foam,
O bitter change from my strong tide of old
That storm-winds drove to darken heaven's dome
When all Poseidon's rank of war unrolled;
But with the wave I wane on sands of saffron.

Now when shy Dawn slips out on feet like silver,
Little I heed her, and my lute is dumb
Whose wont it was to grace her way with song,
Yet I hear even gentler footsteps come,
Nor, when they reach my door, will it be long
Till I go forth in lead who so loved silver.


## KWAN-YIN

To LAURENCE BINYON

Queen of Pity, pure and white,
Poising on the crescent moon
Of a star-enchanted night,
May our prayers with thee have ending
When their silver cloud ascending
Lifts a pillar of pale light!

Lady of Compassion, blest,
Gather the appealing flowers
Of our sorrow up to rest!
Lay them with thy lotus-petals
On whose milky chalice settles
Peace who hovers at thy breast!

Goddess whose enduring brow
Bears the third and mystic eye,
Shed thy loving-kindness now;
Hear us at thy feet inclining,
Show us grace, O pearl of Shining
Bride of Consolation, thou!


## THE BARBERINI FAUN

## To EWAN FRAZER

How heavy weighs the dream upon thy brow;
Could all the wine of Hellas' purple grapes
Bring thee so deep a drowsiness as now
Breathes in the marble murmur that escapes?
Art thou not come by wild and wood-land ways,
At hazard to the very halls of Sleep,
Where Morpheus, making night of all thy days,
Will spill thy golden sands on his gray heap?
Is no light on the verge of that dim land
Wherein thou dwellest? Crowd the dreams so close
That Life may no more stir the drooping hand
Than change thy charmed poppy to a rose?

Then sleep thou, Faun, the sounder for our sake
Who else would lose a wonder, couldst thou wake.

*MUNICH, 1912.*


## SPRING

Crimson, silver, and vair,
Over the edge of the earth,
Shifting, shining, and rare
Comes Beauty to birth.

Green is her mantle afloat,
White the star in her hair,
The rose red at her throat;
Crimson, silver, and vair.


## IN TERRA D' OLTRA MARE

The moon 's high-risen, and the stars all lit,
And here alone I sit:

Alone, that dearest solitude one knows,
When thought takes life and grows.

Out of the darkness, far, from the world's end,
O sudden, wished-for friend!

Out of the silence, over the gray sea,

Yet close, so close to me,

The light and slender shadow of your grace,
Moving before my face!

Still under drooping lashes the dream lies
Softly, upon soft eyes,

Whose hushed delight yourself may scarcely guess,
Stars in a misty dress.

Not yet your beauty, carried like a flower,
Knows all its gift and power;

And still the lips shut close still seem afraid
A thought should be betrayed.

Now, with the world asleep, beneath us blind,
Will you not say your mind?

I called you and you came to me, and here
So soon the dawn draws near.

A moment's speech, a glance, a touch of hands
How well one understands!

Vaya! Across the threshold of the day
Flutters the first, faint ray.


CONQUISTADOR

To MEREDITH STARR (H.C.)

Borne high upon the "billow of largesse"
The mystic, swept across the infinite sea,
Beholds the burning of the sun's excess
On everlasting waters rising free.

No longer perilled in the ocean-rage
Tosses the aimless barque of human hands,
But his strong sails adventurous engage
And bear him upon unimagined lands.

Faint on a verge of unsubstantial cloud
He leaves the shadowed earth of dark desire;
The thunders of eternity are loud,

The sacred air is lit with living fire.

So, in his passage empyrean, steers
The helmsman of the destinies of Man:
In foam before him flake the smitten years,
The winds blow wide the fragments of the plan.

*NOTE. "The billow of largesse hath appeared, the thunder of the sea hath arrived." Jelalu' d' Din (Nicholson's translation).*


## NOCTURNE OF LILIES

On these shy waters where the star-light lingers
I would we might for ever dream afloat,
And music follow us, a silver note;
The wind among the leaves has such soft fingers.

Your thoughts fall in my mind as water falling,
And no word stirs the stillness, yet I hear:
Heart is so close to heart, and Love so near,
Content to listen who was always calling.

Your pale hands move among pale lilies, slowly;
Your hair is like a shadow, and your eyes
Shadowy waters in whose keeping lies
The secret of a region far and holy.

O wise beyond all wisdom born of weeping,
O fairer than all women counted fair,
A child of moon and water, in the rare
Hour when the spirit leaves her prison, sleeping!


## THEME DE BALLET

### To MOLLY MCARTHUR

Dancers by moon-time dance;
Her silver glories glance
Through curtains amber, ivory, and vair,
And not the wind goes lighter
Than their light feet, or whiter
Than their pale hands snow threads the wintry air.

While through the windows dim

A fitful sound and slim
Flits as the rising, falling fountains play,
A cadence faint they borrow
From lands that laugh at Sorrow,
The maiden stealing in a mantle gray.

But soon an elfin choir
From smitten lute and lyre
Conjures a music dizzying and sweet
Whose echoes pierce and tremble,
Are scattered and assemble,
And follow and precede the flying feet.

Like shadows in a glass
The linked, swift lovers pass,
Behind whose speed the dust of their delight,
Now upward twisting, twining,
Climbs in a column shining,
Now breaks and flowers, a lily in the night.

Each for the other's eyes
Can lift the veil that lies
Shading the triumph or the tears of Fate,
Can dip a thought's space under
Her mask of fear and wonder,
And glide between the guardians of her gate.

Like vehement, fine fire
The flames of their desire
Burn clear together, as the rays burn one
Of a rose-opal, blending
All lights to light transcending:
An age, an instant, and the dance is done!


VENICE

The cities of the world have tongues as we
Have; many sounds and colours blend in each;
They in their moods complain, command, beseech,
But one sings her own praise exultantly,
The Siren in the Adriatic Sea.
When her voice echoes there is heard no speech
Over the ever-ringing earth to reach
That choir of triumph in her song set free.

The seasons that go envying renown

Have yielded her all loveliness they hold:
For her the suns rise showering rose and gold,
Scattering purple and silver they go down.
She wears the night as a queen wears her crown,
The waters lift her mantle fold by fold.

### Actaeon
I saw the gleam of the spear of Diana, the huntress;
I heard in a Thracian wood the baying of hounds,
And beside me, fear in his eyes, a stag ran failing,
And I was Actaeon, and died of a thousand wounds.

### Psyche
Love lay asleep, and his dreams, soft, delicate things,
Hovered and murmured over his golden head,
And I was Psyche, and watched their wonderful wings
Till the lamp was shaken, and all the loveliness fled.

### Endymion
Purple night hung over a Latmian valley,
The Moon, my mistress, stooped from her silver throne:
Death, in the kiss, lost all his sting for the sweetness,
And I, Endymion, move where the stars are sown.

### Danae
A mist came down to my tower, all golden gleaming,
And I was loved of the Ruler of Gods thereunder,
Till I woke, Danae, from the dream of my dreaming,
Hearing the wine-dark seas, and the echoing thunder.

White poppies drowse amid pale fields of silence;
Sleep weighs the stooping wheat:
No mortal voice is lifted,
No song of birds comes drifted;
The river winds among the meadows, listening,
And Night has timid feet.

Under the shadow of a drowsing ilex
Love and my soul commune:
Time in the dust is humbled,

Life's laboured walls lie crumbled;
My Self is slain: eternal, with the Eternal,
I breathe my thought in tune.

Peace flutters like a moth against mine eyelids:
"There is no sound," I said . . .
Now golden sounds come stealing
Of singing planets wheeling,
And in the infinite dark the mighty Guardians
Chaunt, and the living dead! . . .


## THE WAY OUT

Gray light, through the windows presently gliding,
Thou wilt discover
Blind Love and blind Hate together abiding,
Slayer and lover:
Coming in peace, peace shalt thou also behold,
Stillness and cold.

Pale Dawn, when thou enterest in to-morrow,
Come with winds wailing,
And rain that has many voices of sorrow
Like flute-notes failing:
Closing the eyes that no more mirror thy light,
Call down the night!


## THE PASSING OF ST NILUS

Soon from my body, a war-worn and soiled sheath,
God, by the pale hand of his henchman Death,
Will draw this blade, my spirit, to lay it by,
Against new need, in his high armoury.
Because I seek no honour in men's thought,
I, who have long but pitifully wrought,
Therefore within these silent walls I sit,
Where none who know my name can honour it.
Out where the white road which the sun loves, goes,
Gay in its borders with the blown wild rose,
Among winds moving ever as they must,
Let a smooth stone cover over my dust,
One giving rest unto wayfaring men
Pilgrims: I also was a pilgrim then.

GRANADA

To BARBARA KNOX

Red walls above the valley,
Calm outpost against Time,
The fabulous Alhambra
Floats in a golden rime.

Day-long the Gate of Justice
Lies wide to brazen feet;
Day-long the throat of clamour
Profanes the hushed retreat:

The pleasure-ground of princes,
The Moslems' ordered grove
Is trodden of intruders,
Drove upon senseless drove.

Despite that passing conquest,
Despite those alien eyes,
The wistful, ancient graces
Still linger and surprise.

The changing "azulejos"
Shine in the dancing sun;
Against their burning facets
The light-rays break and run:

In gleaming courts and spacious
Green waters bear a sky
Whose stirless noon of beauty
Imprisoned seems to lie:

The many-coloured arches
Poise on their marble limbs,
And the crouched, solemn wardens
Drowse by the bason-rims.

Still frames each Moorish window
A slim, fantastic scene
Where white-veiled maidens whisper,
And languorously lean:

Or, when the moon shines silver,
Clear crescent of the Moors,

They lift white arms and praise her,
And still the dream endures.

Red walls above the valley,
Calm outpost against Time,
The fabulous Alhambra
Floats in a golden rime.


## LEYENDA TOLEDANA

A mad king, losing in the stars his thought,
Lives in the wheeling of their golden light,
And no red cloud of ruin round him wrought
Veils the divine, disordered sight;
No voice perturbs his lone communion with the night.

When in the shadow stirred a snake of steel,
How should he listen for the traitor's tread?
His eyes had beauty for a burning seal
And saw her scarlet blossom shed?
The rose of all the skies is gathered for the dead.

Has Night not laid her shroud upon the tower,
Purple and sable that beseem a king?
And Death who entered in a sacred hour,
Behold! had royal gifts to bring!
For peace is on that brow: is peace an evil thing?


## TO TIME, TO HAVE SOFT THOUGHTS TOWARDS NANCY

Fall lightly, fall like flowers'
Shed petals, shining hours,
You that were gladdened in a golden air,
Ripened in silver showers.
Even as wind and dew
Went tenderly to you,
Lie gently, gently on her golden hair!

Slip softly, slip like rays
Through leaves, long summer days!
Made you not merry under opening skies,
And were not woodland ways
Glad of your gliding feet?
Your gift it is to greet;

So, gaily, gaily welcome waking eyes.

Forget, forget thy tears,
Time, thou hast younger years;
Didst thou not dance with dryads in a ring,
And fauns of pointed ears?
Out of that Attic glade
Evoke old music made,
And laughing, laughing, let the echoes sing!


## SPARROW HILL

### To THOMAS WHITTEMORE

THE KINGDOMS OF THE EARTH AND ALL THEIR GLORY!
This were too little, weighed against thy gold,"
Murmured the conqueror, standing alone:
The wonder clutched his heart and he was still,
And silently the tempter set the scene.
Now was the clear air full of magic voices,
And hands unearthly swung the sudden bells;
Tier upon tier of cupolas and domes
The fairy city rose, the holy fortress,
The Kremlin of the river and red walls.
Praise of awakened throats acclaimed the morning
When Death took up his stand on Sparrow Hill.
Never proud eagle, in a mountain-eyrie,
Scanned the sheer crags with such a burning eye
As he who saw that sacred city shining
And leaned with an imperial desire.
For him no gates of legendary Rome
Nor Egypt couchant in her wasted sands
So broke his calm deliberately deep,
But now when keen about his laurelled brows
Blew the chill wind of Fate, and vacant darkness
Closed like a cloud upon his urging mind,
Then he who from no stricken field of Europe
Turned ever with a broken sword subdued
Now, all unwitting, bowed his knees in bondage
And staggered in a viewless victor's train.
No hand wrote redly on a boding sky,
In characters of doom, "The cup is full!"
And down the winding valley of Avernus
Death and the Man of Destiny moved on.

*Moscow, 1912.*

## ON A COLOUR-PRINT OF UTAMARO

To RALPH PHILIPSON

Slanting-eyed and slender-handed,
Utamaro's lady dreams;
Like a sable casque of Pallas
Her inhuman head-dress gleams.
Pure of line and clear and finite,
Balanced like a pallid flower,
Yet her cold, impassive beauty
Changes with no changing hour,
Fanning in a land of fragrance
Star-lit, lonely, and remote,
Silent and serene and soulless,
Ebon hair and silver throat.


## AGAINST DEAD LEAVES

Away, away! Griefs and Austerities
And Wisdom garnering the dust! now lies
The Flower of Life with petals sunward turning,
The Rose of Hope is burning,
And Beauty brims her cup with crimson wine.
Golden, the Sun-God leads the dancing Nine,
And laughing down clear alleys out of shade
Slips Dawn, the saffron Maid.
Bright dew pearls on her gleaming kirtle; song
Gushes from throats that silent were so long:
The feet are glad of swiftness and the eyes
Glad of all loveliness and new surprise,
And who shall sorrow over Autumn leaves?

Blow, Wind! Blow, Wind! and twist the russet sheaves:
Gather and scatter, gay and reckless hands;
The glass is turned and swiftly spill the sands,
And who shall sorrow over Autumn leaves?

Only the gray fool grieves:
Memory, Memory, thou hast long ears
And thou art saddled with a pack of years
I would not bear for all Golconda's bury.
Away, away! The mad horn sounds so merry,

And fleet afoot is Pleasure on the hills,
The quarry no man kills.
The Blue Bird circles in the shining air;
Sunward the wings flash and the bright eyes dare:
Life laughs and Love deceives,
And who shall sorrow over Autumn leaves?


## PERVIGILIUM VENERIS

A bowl of roses and a jar
Of wine

Await what love thou wilt, my star,
Assign.

Thou hastening stranger, do not pass
My door!

The feet that leave, return, alas,
No more.

When hath my silver mirror learned
Deceit?

The grace is mine thy graces burned
To greet.

Hast thou not dreamed of sombre eyes
And deep,

Like waters where a wild light lies
Asleep?

Hast thou not dreamed of kisses like
A flower?

Listen and hear afar Time strike
The Hour!

The lutes are luring in the street
Without

The timid and delaying feet
Of Doubt.

Softly, as when the west winds blow

Soft rain,

Summon my lover, lutes of slow
Refrain!

The door is open; rose and wine
Await,

And yet thou comest, Love of mine,
So late!

The petals of the rose fall, pale
And gray . . .

Now the last stars grow faint and fail
Away . . .

Dawn shakes her torch of saffron fire
And red . . .

And night, ah night, and not desire
Is dead! . . ,


MEMORIAL

I

O quiet hands, O silent feet,
Pale mouth upon whose lips are laid
The lilies of forgetfulness,
White as her heart, eternal Maid.
Calm forehead where the still leaves meet
Of that dark cypress whose caress
To marble lends its perfect shade,
The soul's withdrawal and retreat.


II

Past is that worldly violence,
That beating on the walls of Fate
Of many weak and wounded hands,
Too rude and shapeless to create.
No part was hers in their pretence,
Aloof from these her spirit stands,
Alone she is content to wait,

The seeming darkness her defence.


III

Peace in her hands, peace on her eyes;
The vessel of her years is filled:
Why would ye weep, why would ye weep,
To whom God gave a world to build?
Let song in sorrow's room arise
And Beauty's flying fingers sweep
Her golden strings that are not stilled,
Nor blurred by Death in any wise.


## ALONA

Winds go crying thy name on the misty waters,
"Alona, Alona! Light of the dreamer's eyes!"
East of the Sun and West of the Moon they wander:
On, wild hunters, on where the strange land lies!

Foam falls white at the edge of the amethyst islands;
"Alona, Alona!" The star-light shimmers and spills;
The red, red rowan sings in her rain-wet branches;
Pools of emerald hide in the breast of the hills.

Where are the wardens, Love, of thy sea-swept Fastness?
Alona, Alona, out of the earth-bound airs
We come on the wings of song, with the vision of beauty,
A heart that trembles led by a hope that dares.

We fling thy name in the fire-flecked bowl of the darkness-
"Alona, Alona!" The Great Gods smile on the hour:
Absolved of the seas of Time and Death and Disaster,
Heart to our heart, O dream to our dream give power!

The Lords of Karma loosen our chains in laughter;
A wave flows over the foundered vessel of days.
Life in our hands being laid like a flawless crystal,
Alona, Alona, the souls that are one give praise!


## SONG FROM "LA PRINCESSE ROUGE"

**The Princess**

Love, like a moth, on tender wing
Flutters close to the flame, my heart:
Delicate wanderer, pause and start,
Near and far, in a witless ring.
Dream and desire,
He fans the fire:
Wilt thou die, O pitiful thing!

**The Ladies**
Dream and desire,
And golden fire:
Death is not such a pitiful thing!

**The Princess**
Love, like a moth, on softest wing
Looks and longs for the star, my soul:
Silver venturer, far thy goal;
Circle, circle, and climb and cling!

**Icy daughter**
Of Moon and Water,
Canst thou bear that desolate thing?

**The Ladies**
Gleaming daughter
Of Moon and Water,
Death is not such a desolate thing.


VISION

I saw a towering shape beside me stand
With a white lily in his lifted hand;
The smile upon his lips was hard to read,
His brows were like inscrutable, smooth sand.

I saw my days go by me in a dream;
My deeds went drifting, straws upon a stream:
I had no will, but watched the wind and tide,
And all the checkered play of gloom and gleam.

Then, last, a cavern darkly came to sight
That swallowed stream and straws, and shade and light
The silent watcher let his lily fall,
And lo, it lay between us, black as night!

I cried, "O slayer of the changing flower,

Though all forgotten time be in thy power,
The spirit flies beyond thy hands; O Death,
Thou hast no harvest of the unborn hour!"

## ROUCOULEMENT

### To FREDERIC MANNING

With what a meditative, cool content
The ring-doves murmur under their wavering roof,
While the sun steps with his quiver well-nigh spent
And with unstrung bow on his shoulders, homeward bent.

Some touch of the same secure indifference,
Reticent, gentle, and quietly held aloof,
Comes to me, bringing a faint and an alien sense
Of Life's perplexities lulled in a like suspense.

The amber over the hills is lit with green:
The twisting smoke climbs up to it out of the town
And swims transfigured in whorls of delicate sheen:
My gray thoughts follow till both are no longer seen.

Even the doves are silent now, and the shade
Over the terraces widens lazily down,
Slips through the porch and sleeps in the soft colonnade:
While in the garden the ghosts go out unafraid.


## THE CHILDREN OF THE SPHINX

### To "HAJJI BABA," A CHINCHILLA TABBY

*"Ame voilee, egoiste, hautaine et parfois indulgente"*

To and fro, on velvet feet,
Move the children of the Sphinx,
Enigmatic and discreet:

They whose slanting vision links
Time to Time's forgotten sires
Till our vaunted wisdom sinks

Shamed against those topaz fires,
And that emerald's sacred flame,
Where the ironic soul admires

Who we are and whence we came,
Creatures of a paltry birth,
Cyphers in the cosmic game,

Graceless cumberers of earth.
So they pass like shadows fleet,
Shadows conscious of their worth,

To and fro on velvet feet.


## SERENADE

In the silver even,
Love, the gentle-eyed,
Came with timid sandals
Where the lawns are wide,
And the owls were calling,
"Night, the night is falling."

At the dearest window
Where the ivy twines,
The beloved, leaning,
Heard the lilted lines,
Caught the music falling,
"Night, the night is calling."


## AUBADE

What thoughts to send you, dear, from these
High-arched, sun-loving trees,
Where the morning wakes and the crisp air sings
In floating bubbles and fugitive rings,
And children's voices and voices of birds
Say the same wise words!

Does the world go well with you? Flash me back
Your answer over the airy track
Our thoughts wear smooth from heart to heart
When our lips must part.

Does the world go well? Are the hills as green
From the cypress-grove, if you peep between,
As when last we looked? Do the woods still sleep
And hold that silence they use to keep
When we get lost in them, hand in hand,
And they understand?

But why send thoughts, you are with me here,
And over my shoulder see just as clear
The shadowy valley, the shining plain,
The flat, red roofs washed bright by the rain,
And the twin gray towers that point to the skies
Like a snail's two horns, with a snail's two eyes;
Then the blue-gray distance, filmy and pale,
And for me no more; can you lift that veil?


## CYCLONE

With all thine anger thou couldst not withhold me, Sea,
With all thy waters shouldering mountain-high,
With the whirling eddy of winds that are in thy fee,
And with noon made night in the shaken, terrible sky.

Though the vessel staggered and plunged like a wounded steed
And the race of the screws flung up into foam and air,
Thy wrath and thy strength were spent, or thy heart gave heed,
And calm came down on the ways of the waves made fair.

Was not a voice in thy tumult heard, and a face
Seen like a star in the wrack of the driving cloud?
One was beside me and we held speech for a space,
And fear went out like a hound that is suddenly cowed.

Not against her are thy hands availing, Sea;
Thou art one, but the Fates that have bound us— Three.


## MEMORY

Memory, embalmer of my fugitive days,
In a wrought urn of silver, white and tall,
Thy touch austere and sacramental lays
Each momentary rose, purpureal.

At the pale lips the mounted fragrance clings,

Summoning up the sense rejuvenate,
Till the lost loves hover on petalled wings
That have long lain folded, inanimate.


## APRIL IN THE ARABIAN SEA

Swift, sweet month of the irised wings, the homeward bearing,
Month of the opal, azure, and varying gold,
April not of the rains nor the northern cold,
Full-blossomed, radiant, saving nowise nor sparing,
Giver of suns by day and of moons by night,
Moons and miraculous stars over infinite waters,
Leading the dance of the days thy unmurmuring daughters.
Bountiful April, lady of laughter and light,
Songs fall faint on the lips that would hymn thee duly,
Is not the voice best heard in the following wind,
In the plash at the prow, in the furrow suddenly lined?
April, these for thy praise, and the white crests rising unruly!


## SOL COUCHANT

The sun is sleeping, dear, I wonder
What dreams creep under
His golden lids and his lashes golden,
What unbeholden
Horror or unsuspected rapture
Closed can they capture?

Does he feel the cool, slow-flowing ocean,
Breathe in the motion
When the great shapes go gleaming, gliding,
Of sea-beasts riding
Tritons upon their dolphins steering,
Green in the mere-ring?

Does a music come to him dimly-breathed
Of sea-shells wreathed?
Does he catch a glimmer of silver-throated
Nereids floated
Up from their sea-deep, echoing chamber
In conches of amber?

Does the light of the risen moon come peeping
Where he lies sleeping?

Her who reigns, with his day's-reign over,
Does night discover;
Does gold from her fingers slip, from her star-train splendid,
As she moves attended?

Does he feel the rush of warrior winds engaging,
Of waters raging?
Does he know when a ship goes down, her timbers straining,
Goes down complaining?
Does he wake to the sound of far-off voices sighing,
Of the drowning dying?

## JOUR DE FETE

To-day the world's new made,
Gold light, green shade,
And behind and over, a pale, deep, limitless blue,
Almost the Tuscan hue,
But a thought softer, kindlier — for you.

Moreover we have banned
Out the five gates of this loud-laughing land
All trees that stoop too much, whose branches fall,
Or whose aspect funereal
Brings, with a sober vesture, sombre thought.
But we have rather sought
Those in whose veins there runs the rich excess
Of their youth's happiness:
Who stay not, sighing in an undertone,
With a burthen moan on moan,
But whose soft leaves, to the wind's pipe set dancing,
Clutch at the sun-rays glancing,
Snare ev'ry side-long sprite:
While to that wanton time
Their voices lilt in an uneven rhyme,
Half mockery, half madness, all delight.

## ENVOI

So much in honour to the day starred white
In the sealed annals whereby Love records
Chance good or evil, and awards
Praise, as him seemeth right.

## THE GRAY CITY

Seeing thee so, under familiar skies
Of clouds slow-moving and soft-falling rain,
No link is loosed of the continual chain
That binds our first and latest destinies.
Seeing thee so, all unremembered eyes,
All places that have long forgotten lain,
Awake to life; they will not sleep again,
Or, should they sleep, would hear thy call, "Arise!"

By the gray meadows of the withered sedge,
Along the lonely curves again I glide
To gather in a month forlorn of flowers
Blossom of old dreams by the wan waves' edge,
To overhear the whispered speech beside,
And shy, returning feet of ancient hours.

## INVOCATION

My thoughts, upon such wings as will you bear,
Go to her now, if ever, for she stands
Lone at the midmost of the lonely lands,
And the sun burns her through the cloudless air.
Go to her now, if ever; bend and share
Her sorrows, and in lieu of clasped hands,
Murmur Love's words through all the ruined sands,
And echo them, ye winds that lift her hair.

Roll swiftly, O thou harsh, dividing sphere,
And spur thy laggard seasons ; shake the reins
Out on the neck of every month that strains
The twelve-fold yoke of this deliberate year;
Then loosen from our days thy grudging hold,
And yield us one to other, as of old.

## FOOL'S SONG

I care not, I,
Though all men pass me blindly;
So she look kindly
Why, let the world go by,
I care not, I.

I care not, I,
Though Fame the jade betray me,
Her lips repay me:
Fame, an you will, good-bye,
I care not, I.

I care not, I,
Though Death the jester flout me:
Her arms about me,
This will be life, to die,
I care not, I.


## DEIRDRE

There is death beyond in the darkness,
His feet move on the wind,
A deep grave dug in the darkness,
Death before and behind.

Soon shall the golden hair be rusted,
The red lips pale wherefore they lusted,
And the bright eyes be blind.

Long after, when all these lie sleeping,
Shall their tale be told over, weeping,
And their ways wake to mind.

There is life beyond even darkness,
His wings beat up the wind;
Love and light beyond the darkness,
Before death and behind.


## CAR TU DEMEURES

You did not leave me when you turned to go;
You did not leave me, no.

Your voice is with me yet, and clear and sweet
Shuts out the crowded street.

Beside the hearth, the cushions of your chair
Remember yet your hair.

And where your foot has touched the fender, see!
The firelight laughs to me.

You did not leave me when you turned to go;
Love cannot leave me so.


## MARGARITAE

Perla mia, O white, light maid,
What Gods gave thee to what prayer prayed;
What star danced in the noon of night
For thy proud birth-right?
Did the Graces meet in the saffron shade,
With shy feet skirting the dew-soft glade,
While she, their mother, left lone somewhile
Sea-girt Cypris and Cnidos Isle;
For sure none other
Than Eros' mother,
Of mingled mist and of pale star-shine,
Made such eyes and such eye-lids thine?
Did Dian float like a moon-moth low
To dower thy lips with her curving bow,
And Hermes fit to those twinkling feet
Two plumes plucked from his sandals fleet?
Did grave Demeter, when thou wert born,
Give thee the glint of her ripening corn
And touch thy locks with the wayward gold
They squander and hold?
Did pale Persephone's twilight flower
Cool thy brows in a stolen hour?
Perla mia, O white, light maid,
Let be the givers, the gifts have stayed!


## GREEN

To EZRA POUND

O thou most various and delicate
Raiment of all things fugitive and frail,
Green — of the first spears quivering and pale,
To Spring's adorning newly recreate;
Green, who dost lend thy mutable estate
To waters wavered when the windy sail
Dips, and the prows uplift the foaming veil,

And the sun follows down the glistening spate.

So laughing; but thou hast thy mysteries,
Green, when the dusk comes shadowed up the lawn,
And softly is thy darker mantle drawn,
And thou art in a mood for mournful eyes:
Then sorrows wait, as on a widowed queen,
About thy passage, hushed and sable Green.


## INANIA

Why weep ye when ye close
The cold eyes of the dead,
Seeing the spirit goes
Forth on a fragile thread,
And why seek now to awaken
The house dark and forsaken?

Why bring ye flowers to lay,
And waste their sweetness blown
Where none have joy, and they
Parch on the carven stone?
This is in vain, bestowing
Gifts on the grave, unknowing.

Why will ye bow your knees,
Taking for God one Death,
Who neither hears nor sees,
Moves, nor is filled with breath?
Life is a flame unending,
Is a swift flame ascending.


## VOYAGE EN ESPANGE

To MRS H. H. CHAMPION

Underneath the beechen shade,
Dark and sparsely lit
By a young moon-crescent swayed
Gray leagues over it;
From the city's waning lights,
Down a winding lane,
On the hazard chance invites
We set out for Spain.

We took no money in our purse,
No staff was in our hand;
Faith, for better or for worse,
In the fabled land
Bade us leave the world behind,
Leave the cares of men;
Fortune loves the trusting mind,
Springs to blossom then.

Winds blew cool, and stars came near;
Sounds that sleep by day
Woke to music frail and clear,
Luring us away.
Like a running stream the miles
Slipped beneath our feet;
When the open road beguiles
Time forgets to fleet.

Up the hills and down the vales
(How I cannot tell),
Like a phantom ship that sails,
Driven by a spell,
To a Spanish port we came
On that night of May,
And the castles dear to fame
Towered above the bay.

You had yours and I had mine,
Each his heart's desire,
Battlements in serried line,
Pinnacle and spire.
Through the frowning porch I passed
Though the gates were barred,
Till I found my dream at last
In my castle-yard.

Friend, when I come home again
(Ah! the months are slow),
We will travel back to Spain
By the road you know:
It is always open wide,
None to take a toll,
When we journey side by side,
Speaking each his soul.

## WHEN LOVE WILL DIE

Let there be no one watching by the bed
When Love will die,
No mourner come with soft and solemn tread
And thither bring remembering flowers to shed,
When Love will die.

But let me sit alone and no tear fall,
No eye grow dim,
And watch the shadows dancing on the wall;
These be for mutes to mock the funeral,
Gray shapes and grim.

Let me not wake the old delights and muse
Upon this death,
And make no vain denial or excuse,
Grieve or regret; these things are little use,
Mere idle breath.

But let me even in the dark hour know,
Since Love has passed,
Love is a light thing that the wind may blow
Hither or thither, but the soul not so;
The soul laughs last.


## LOST VOICES

### To LIONEL LINDSAY

There is a sound of lutes along the wind,
An old, lost music, blurred and seeming blind,
At dusk between the branches. So it sings
Of many ancient, unremembered things,
Of lovers and their loves that lie behind
Time, in the shadow of his fallen wings.

Songs in the wind's mouth, shall I bid you flower;
Buds, shall I call you to your opening hour,
Twine in new garlands with a bygone sweet
Touch as of sundered lips that no more meet?
Songs in the wind's mouth, shall I wake your power
Now for a new love, to a new heart's beat?

## HEIMKEHRER'S-LIED

Now, when the fluted songs of spring
Are in all your fresh and awakening ways,
With a clear, undoubtable, elfin ring
Of the silver herald of revelling days,
Here to me in the ever-green,
Never-green,
Sun-glutted gardens of withering hue,
Comes, eyes shut and my thoughts run free,
A primrose glimmer of over the sea;
Of the banks of the beeches that look to the blue
Sky shed mistily, witchingly new,
To the sound of the song of the months that is blown,
"We follow, we follow the footsteps flown!
Moon, moon, of the May-time,
Play-time,
Laughing sickle of mellowing hours,
Soon, soon is thy reaping,
O white one sleeping
Through April weeping,
A mother of flowers!"


## TRUE EYES

True eyes
Being given to Memory's keeping,
Of the unfading, the tender light,
Shine for me though all stars be sleeping!
Though the sky blinds you, weeping,
Quietly, in the clouds' despite,
Answer my spirit's sight,
True eyes.
When I am gone out in the night
With the long and the gray waves sweeping,
Give me to reach your height,
As I would, as I might,
True eyes.


## ON A COLOUR-PRINT BY TORIL KIYONAGA

### To MRS H. C. MARRYAT

The frailest beauties of the Yoshiwara

With slender fingers play on the samisen,
While through their latticed balcony the moon looks,
Pale, with her faint face of a floated lily ;
And the long shadows take the paths of silence
Over the marge of the Sumida river.


## CAMARADERIE

Space and a silence, the eternal friends,
Hold us, we have no need of lesser hands,
And night, when night descends,
Understands.

Our subtleties are not profaned of speech:
When Time was nameless we were close of kin,
Our language each to each
Heard within.

Birth and re-birth through all the cycle-change
Leave us immutable our ancient tongue,
The mystical, the strange,
Ever-young.

Men's momentary laughter on the wind
Passes beside us like a driven leaf,
Blows too, beyond, their blind,
Fickle grief:

Silence and Space and shadow-mantled Night
Commune with us, the primal verities,
And the stars' lonely light
Fills our eyes.


## AMOUR VOYAGEUR

I can scarce hear the singing of the wind
For her voice that sings in mine ear;
Stay waves, and thou, wind, be still,
Let me listen my fill,
Sleep ye, she is near.

That was her hand came stealing into mine,
Are her ways not subtle, not wise?
Gray Time, wilt thou venture between,

Is thy sickle as keen,
Gray Time, as her eyes?


## BUDDHA

### To MRS SHAKESPEAR

Red of red gold and dusk of bronze,
Ananda's Lord his lotus-throne
Holds, and the rhythmic orisons
About him break as waters blown
When dark goes down on ocean shores.
His calm and solemn-lidded eyes,
Beyond the gloom of guarded doors,
Beyond the cloudy centuries,
Watch, without wearying, the light
That shone before the stars were sown,
Or were divided day and night,
That light wherein the end is known.


## RONDEL FOR THE NIGHT

Good-night the wind is crying, and a cloud
Between me and the moon of my delight
Drifts, and I lean and watch it, sullen-browed,
Good-night.

Once, even so, was hidden from my sight
Your soul that took a heavy thought for shroud,
And changed for sable her untainted white.

Long though I leaned and called your name aloud,
And Echo heard, you did not hear me right,
And my lips faltered and my head was bowed
Good-night.